SECRETS HIDDEN WITHIN

THE LEVI COFFIN HOUSE

Bouncing up and down, shaken left and right.

Jarred by holes in the road and lying on a hard plank of wood.

They were cold, hungry, scared, and exhausted, but hopefully this journey on the Underground Railroad would lead them to a safe house and eventually to freedom.

Hidden underneath straw and bags of grain, the runaway slaves dared not make a sound.

Would they make it or would they be captured and sent back to their owners?

Later that night, Levi and Catharine Coffin were awaken by knocking at their door. The Coffins were used to being awakened in the middle of the night by travelers of the Underground Railroad, since fugitive slaves traveled at night in order to make escape easier. Some times the conductors would arrive with passengers in horse and buggy, some times on foot.

From outside, Levi and Catharine's house looked pretty much like others. However inside, the house held many secrets.

The Coffin's cellar was dug very deep. It is quite unusual to have a kitchen located in the cellar. Notice the stairs. Often fugitives would enter the house here.

Since fugitives were wanted by the law, they needed to be hidden. There were no windows here. Noise would not carry far. One of the first things runaways needed was food, so this was the perfect place to begin talking to and aiding them.

Fugitives could be hidden in a feather bed for a short period of time. A feather bed is lumpy thus making it easy to hide someone. Two girls were concealed here once, but got to giggling and had to be separated. Has that ever happened to you when you stayed at someone else's house? It would be very dangerous, if you were hiding.

Levi and Catharine's house had several places to hide runaways. A piece of furniture could hide a doorway in this room.

When the bed was slid over, the doorway would be covered. Through the doorway is an area between the walls where many people could hide. Most of the runaways were not young children. Why would age be an issue?

Did you say that it is hard for young children to keep up with the pace and the distance they would have to travel and also to hide quietly? That is correct.

Can you imagine living in a tiny space for two weeks and not being able to come out to eat, play, or use the bathroom, and having to keep quiet?

Catharine would carry food to people hidden in the house in a basket with freshly ironed clothing on top. Fugitives were seldom allowed to eat in the kitchen after arrival, because they must stay safely hidden. Sometimes the Coffins had guests and servants in the house, so the need for secrecy was always needed.

There was no running water inside the house. Most people used wells or springs with the pump outside the house similar to the one below. The Coffins put their well inside their house, which was not a common practice. How would that help hide fugitives?

By not going outside their house to get water, the Coffins could keep secret the amount of water being used. The more people, the more water was needed.

If someone were watching and noticed many trips to get water, more than was needed for the number of known people in the house, the watcher would become suspicious.

Since many fugitives arrived with no belongings and the clothing they had was dirty and in tatters, the Coffins had to find ways to clothe them. This is the sewing room where Catharine and a group of ladies formed a sewing circle. They make clothing and kept it until they needed it.

The Underground Railroad was not really a railroad, but an underground (secret) resistance. It was the secret routes for African-American slaves to escape to free states or to Canada.

LEVI COFFIN

Levi Coffin (1798-1877), a Quaker abolitionist, lived in Newport (now Fountain City) with his family 1826-1847. Moved from North Carolina because he and his wife, Catharine, opposed slavery. Advocated, and sold in his store, free-labor products not produced by slaves. House built circa 1839; designated a National Historic Landmark 1966.

(Continued on other side)

ROUTES FROM SOUTH TO NORTH ALONG THE UNDERGROUND RAILROAD.

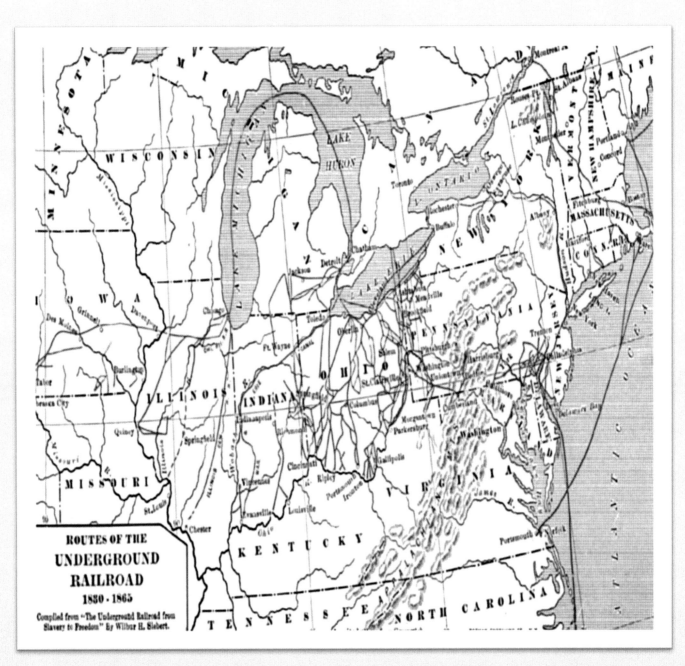

Notice how the routes into Illinois, Indiana, and Ohio begin along the line of the river. The banks of the Ohio River in these states was the border of the free states.

Many runaways who Levi and Catharine helped, crossed into the free state of Indiana, through Louisville, Kentucky. The fugitives had to cross the Ohio River. Usually they had no boat. There is a story about a lady crossing on frozen ice. Some fugitives were hidden on steamboats.

The Coffin's were Quakers and they did not believe in slavery. They began providing shelter to run away slaves in the winter of 1826-27.   Here's a quote from Levi in his book, *Reminiscences*.

"Soon after we located at Newport, I found that we were on a line of the U.G.R.R. [Underground Railroad].... I was willing to receive and aid as many fugitives as were disposed to come to my house. I knew that my wife's feelings and sympathies regarding this matter were the same as mine, and that she was willing to do her part...."

LEVI COFFIN, REMINISCENCES OF LEVI COFFIN (CINCINNATI, 1876)

Members of The Underground Railroad Movement used names of the transportation system for the process of helping runaways. The station master was the person who hid the runaways. The fugitives were the cargo, and the group of fugitives and conductor were the train. People leading the men and women to safety were called conductors. The horse was called the locomotive. The safe house was the station.

When a station master was ready to send the train on up the line, sometimes they sent coded messages.

Here is one of those messages:

I have sent via at two o'clock four large hams and two small hams.

CLUES: hams are people
       via means on the Underground Railroad

How did you do?

The message means:
I have sent on the
Underground Railroad
at 2 o'clock, four
adults and two
children.

TRY THIS ONE!

> *I have sent via at midnight, one adult bull and two heifers.*

Did you say?
I have sent on the Underground Railroad at midnight, one adult male and two young females.

Why would the station masters talk about horses, hams, and cows instead of computers, tractors, and magnetic slime?

Computers, tractors, and magnetic slime were not invented yet. They used things that were commonly traded in that time era. What other things might be used in a coded message from that time era?

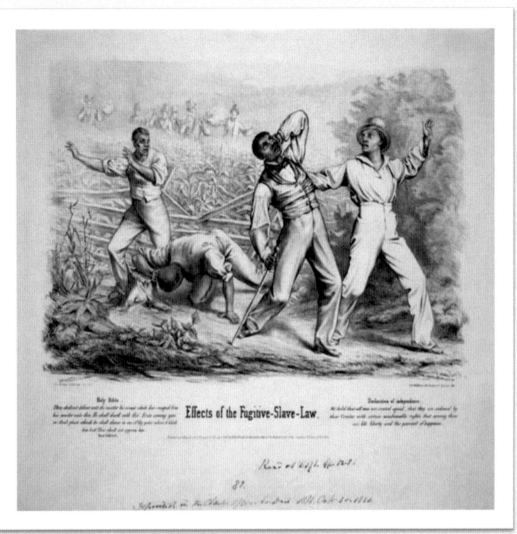

It was very dangerous for Levi and Catharine to provide a safe house, because of the Fugitive Slave Act of 1850. By law, any runaway slaves had to be returned to their owner. Anyone not doing so faced a huge fine and imprisonment. Levi said he thought they helped about one hundred slaves escape a year.

How did the Coffins manage to help so many people escape slavery? They were resourceful in outsmarting runaway slaves. They made modifications to their house so they could hide people. But, they were still breaking the law.

This is the stairs leading from outside into the kitchen cellar.

Levi Coffin

Does this person look like he'd break the law?

Catharine Coffin

What about this lady?

This is what the Fugitive Slave Law of 1850 said:

1. **Any citizen was required to catch runaway slaves.**
2. **If a person did not do so, they could be fined up to $1,000 or put in jail for six months.**

Many Northerners hated this law because they had to help out the system of slavery or be in violation of the law.

By helping runaway slaves, the Coffins were breaking this law and faced the punishment.

Imagine a runaway knocking on your door late at night. What would you think was happening? Would you help them? Where would you hide the fugitive? How would you clothe them and help them on their way?

If Levi had fugitives who needed to leave his house, but slave hunters were looking for them, how could he disguise them? What would you do?

Some times fugitives were dressed in the unexpected. Women might be dressed as men or young boys. Men would be dressed as women. One runaway was dressed in elegant clothing, another dressed as a mother with a child. These often threw off slave hunters who often did not know what the person looked like they were hunting.

It might be easier to disguise people today since we have more means of changing faces with makeup and using wigs.

How does what Levi and Catharine did compare to the issue with immigration today? What should happen to people who illegally cross the border into the United States? Should they be sent back, arrested, or given jobs?

More information about the Levi Coffin House can be found on their facebook page:
https://www.facebook.com/search/top/?q=Levi%20Coffin%20House

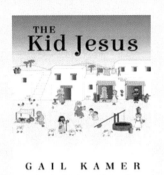

THE
Kid Jesus

GAIL KAMER

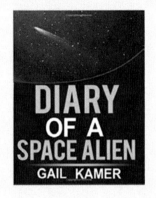

DIARY
OF A
SPACE ALIEN
GAIL KAMER

WHAT IS
THAT THING?

GAIL KAMER

Chick
-A-
Bunga

Gail Kamer
Illustrated by Matt Real

THE PARDON
BY GAIL KAMER

BEACH
BIRDS

GAIL KAMER

FANG SANG

By Gail Kamer
Illustrated By Sandy Hardin

Swoosh and Slide
Search and Glide

Gail Kamer
Illustrator--Matt Real

Thank you for purchasing Secrets Hidden Within the Levi Coffin House. Here are some of my other books.

My books can be found on Amazon.com

Made in the USA
Monee, IL
12 June 2024

59790160R00019